Kids Talk About
Bravery

by Carrie Finn illustrated by Amy Bailey Muehlenhardt

Special thanks to our advisers for their expertise:

Dr. Kay Herting Wahl, Director of School Counseling
University of Minnesota

Susan Kesselring, M.A., Literacy Educator
Rosemount–Apple Valley–Eagan Minnesota School District

PiCTURE WiNDOW BOOKS
Minneapolis, Minnesota

Editor: Christianne Jones

Designer: Joe Anderson

Page Production: Brandie Shoemaker

Editorial Director: Carol Jones

Creative Director: Keith Griffin

The illustrations in this book were created digitally.

Picture Window Books

5115 Excelsior Boulevard

Suite 232

Minneapolis, MN 55416

877-845-8392

www.picturewindowbooks.com

Printed in the United States of America.

Photo Credit: Bettmann/Corbis, page 30

Library of Congress Cataloging-in-Publication Data

Finn, Carrie.

Kids talk about bravery / by Carrie Finn ; illustrated by Amy Bailey Muehlenhardt.

p. cm. – (Kids talk jr.)

Includes bibliographical references and index.

ISBN-13: 978-1-4048-2314-3 (hardcover)

ISBN-10: 1-4048-2314-X (hardcover)

1. Courage—Juvenile literature. I. Muehlenhardt, Amy Bailey, 1974- II. Title. III. Series.

BJ1533.C8F56 2006   2006003398

179'.6–dc22

Kids Talk Jr.

COUNSELOR: Kendra

Hi, Friends!

My name is Kendra Kemp. I'm in the fifth grade at Newton Elementary School. My friends call me "Kind Kendra." My favorite thing to do is to give advice and help others.

Bravery is when you face the things that scare you. Sometimes it's hard to be brave. Read on and see what I have to say about being brave.

Sincerely,

Kendra

Dear Kendra,

I am scared of a dog that lives by our house. What can I do?

Jesse

Kids Talk Jr.

COUNSELOR: Kendra

Dear Jesse,

Part of being brave is facing your fears. Have an adult go with you to visit the dog and its owner. I bet the dog is scared of you, too.

Kendra

Dear Kendra,

My mom told me that I have to go to the doctor to get a shot. I'm scared. What should I do?

Molly

Kids Talk Jr.

COUNSELOR: Kendra

Dear Molly,

Remember, shots help keep you healthy. Your mom will be with you the whole time. It's easier to be brave when someone is with you.

Kendra

Dear Kendra,

Sometimes I'm afraid during the night. What can I do so I don't get scared?

Riley

Kids Talk Jr.

COUNSELOR: Kendra

Dear Riley,

I think everyone gets a little scared during the night. I keep a flashlight by my bed. If I get scared, I turn it on and check things out.

Kendra

Dear Kendra,

My soccer coach wants me to be the goalie for the next game.
I don't know if I can do it. What should I do?

Thomas

Kids Talk Jr.

COUNSELOR: Kendra

Dear Thomas,

Doing something you've never done before takes bravery. Just keep your eyes on the ball and try your hardest. Good luck!

Kendra

Dear Kendra,

I get nervous when I talk to my grandma. She's so much older than I am. What should I talk about?

Jill

Kids Talk Jr.

COUNSELOR: Kendra

Dear Jill,

Talk to your grandma like you would talk to your friends. Tell her stories about your life. I'll bet she will share some fun stories, too.

Kendra

Dear Kendra,

Our class is having a spelling bee on Friday. I get scared standing up in front of people. What can I do?

Logan

Kids Talk Jr.

COUNSELOR: Kendra

Dear Logan,

It will be easier to be brave if you feel prepared for the spelling bee. Study hard and do your best. Just pretend you are in your room practicing all alone. Good luck!

Kendra

...f...a...i...n..t...

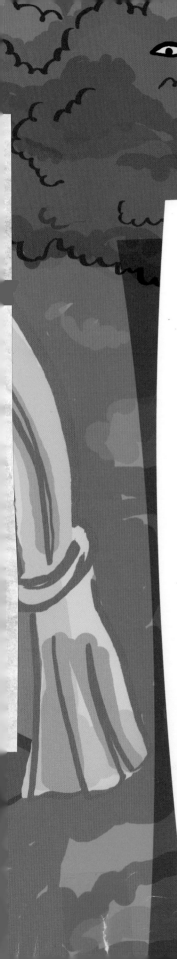

Dear Kendra,

My cousin Abby invited me to go camping with her family. Will there be scary animals out there?

Becca

Kids Talk Jr.

COUNSELOR: Kendra

Dear Becca,

The animals are probably just as scared of you as you are of them. Knowing this will help you feel brave. Remember, the animals are sharing their home with you.

Kendra

Dear Kendra,

I stole some candy from the store, and now I have to take it back. I'm scared! What should I do?

Clark

Kids Talk Jr.

COUNSELOR: Kendra

Dear Clark,

It's hard to tell someone that you've done something wrong. The store owner will respect your bravery when you tell the truth. However, you should be punished for shoplifting.

Kendra

Dear Kendra,

I want to jump off the high diving board at the local pool, but I'm scared. Am I a chicken?

Luther

Kids Talk Jr.

COUNSELOR: *Kendra*

Dear Luther,

Take it in steps. First, jump off the side of the pool. Then, jump off the low diving board. Soon you'll be ready to jump off the high board. Have fun!

Kendra

Dear Kendra,

My sister is in the Army. People say she is brave. Why do they say that?

Ryan

Kids Talk Jr.

COUNSELOR: Kendra

Dear Ryan,

It takes lots of bravery to stand up for something you believe in and to protect your country. Your sister believes in freedom and in defending that freedom. A lot of people are thankful for her brave work.

Kendra

Kids Talk Jr.

COUNSELOR: Kendra

That's all the time I have for today. I have to get to dance class. I hope I answered all of your questions about being brave. Turn the page and learn more about bravery!

Sincerely,

Kendra

Grab a piece of paper and a pencil, and take this fun quiz. Good luck!

1. Getting a shot is
    a) super fun.
    b) not fun at all, but it's easier to be brave if someone
       goes with you.
    c) the coolest thing ever.

2. If you are scared of a dog, you should
    a) have your mom or dad go with you to meet the dog's owner.
    b) bark loudly at the dog.
    c) run away from the dog.

3. The scary things in your bedroom are
    a) monsters.
    b) pigs.
    c) just shadows.

4. To help you be more brave when playing soccer, you should
   keep your eyes on the
    a) ball.
    b) sky.
    c) umbrellas.

5. When you talk to your grandma, you should
    a) tell her about your life.
    b) tell her lies.
    c) not say anything.

6. To get ready for a spelling bee, you should
   a) hold your breath as long as possible.
   b) draw a picture of your house.
   c) study your spelling words and practice.

7. Animals are scared of
   a) people.
   b) ice cream.
   c) hot dogs.

8. If you admit to stealing something, you are
   a) tall.
   b) brave.
   c) a clown.

9. Diving boards can be
   a) purple with green spots.
   b) scary if you've never jumped off one before.
   c) underwater.

10. It's important to be thankful for people who serve in the
   a) Army.
   b) circus.
   c) zoo.

Ruby Bridges

Ruby Bridges became a hero when she was only 6 years old. In 1960, Ruby became the first African American child to go to an all-white school in New Orleans. At this time, black children and white children went to different schools.

When Ruby got to school, there were hundreds of people waiting for her. Many of them weren't happy that she was going to be allowed to go to school there. Some of them shouted at her and called her names.

Ruby didn't miss a day of school. She didn't cry and or act scared when people yelled at her. She showed everyone that she could be brave.

Glossary

advice—suggestions about what to do about a problem

bravery—having courage

confidence—to trust in a person or thing

favorite—something you like better than any other

hero—someone who has courage, strength, and does things that other people can't do

impossible—something that can't be done

punish—to make a person suffer for something he or she did wrong

To Learn More

AT THE LIBRARY

Cocca-Leffler, Maryann. *Bravery Soup.* Morton Grove, Ill.: A Whitman, 2002.

Hirschmann, Kris. *Courage.* Chicago: Raintree, 2004.

Moncure, Jane Belk. *The Child's World of Courage.* Plymouth, Minn.: Child's World, 1997.

ON THE WEB

FactHound offers a safe, fun way to find Internet sites related to this book.

All of the sites on FactHound have been researched by our staff.

1. Visit *www.facthound.com*
2. Type in this special code for age-appropriate sites: 140482314X
3. Click on the FETCH IT button.

Your trusty FactHound will fetch the best sites for you!

Index

Look for all of the books in the Kids Talk Jr. series:

Kids Talk About Bravery	1-4048-2314-X
Kids Talk About Bullying	1-4048-2315-8
Kids Talk About Fairness	1-4048-2316-6
Kids Talk About Honesty	1-4048-2317-4
Kids Talk About Respect	1-4048-2318-2
Kids Talk About Sharing	1-4048-2319-0